One Size Cloth Diaper
Pattern

Copyright 2012 Mammacandoit.com

This page is intentionally blank

Visit www.mammacandoit.com for downloadable PDF patterns

One Size Diaper Pattern - Index

1. Diaper Cover Page
2. Index
3. Supplies & Hints
4. Diaper Tutorial Step 1-4
5. Diaper Tutorial Step 5-8
6. Diaper Tutorial Step 9-12
7. Diaper Tutorial Step 13-16
8. Diaper Tutorial Step 17 & 18
9. Optional Gussets Tutorial Step 1-3
10. Optional Gussets Tutorial Step 4-7
11. Optional Adjustable Elastic Tutorial Step 1-3
12. Optional Adjustable Elastic Tutorial Step 4-5
13. Tips & Tricks
14. Diaper Pattern Piece A
15. Diaper Pattern Piece B
16. Diaper Pattern Piece C
17. Insert Cover Page
18. Insert Tutorial Step 1-2
19. Insert Tutorial Step 3-8

This page is intentionally blank

Visit www.mammacandoit.com for downloadable PDF patterns

Unlocking Creativity | You can do it.

Copyright 2012 Mammacandoit.com

One Size Diaper
Pattern

WHAT YOU NEED:

<u>Outer Layer</u>
   PUL - 18x20"
<u>Hidden layer for snap backing</u>
   PUL - 10x15"
<u>Inner layer</u>
   Alova -18x20"
<u>Elastic</u>
   3 - 6" pieces of 1/4" braided elastic
   (*Optional page 9*) 9 snap sockets & 3 snap studs
<u>Snap down front</u>
   9 snap sockets
   3 snap studs
<u>Closure</u>
   10 x 1.5" loop (velcro) or 20 snap sockets
   2 - 2x1" hook (velcro) or 4 snap studs
<u>Tools</u>
   Polyester thread
   Fabric marking pen or chalk
   Yardstick or ruler
   Sewing Machine

HINTS:

<u>Outer Layer:</u>
PUL is a leakproof barrier and it is what we recommend. However, if you have a separate cover, flannel will work well for this layer.
<u>Hidden layer for snap backing:</u>
Some people choose to skip this step. We recommend that you do not skip. This layer helps the snaps to stay in a sturdy place as well as keeps any 'wicking' from happening around the snaps and/or velcro. You could use Nylon instead of PUL.
<u>Inner Layer:</u>
We recommend Alova because it is a thin, moisture wicking fabric that will draw moisture away from the skin and into the soaker. It is polyester. If you wish to make the diaper with cotton against the skin, substitute the alova with flannel.
<u>Elastic:</u>
The optional snaps are for adjustable elastic. This is handy if the cloth diapers will be used on newborns. However, since children are all different shapes and sizes, we recommend the adjustable elastic even when newborns will not be wearing.
<u>Snap down front:</u>
Typically people use resin or plastic snaps.
<u>Closure:</u>
Choose to use hook & loop (velcro) or snaps. For this diaper, we recommend using hook and loop because it is more customizable to your child's size as they are growing.

SNAPS FOR A BEGINNER:

STUD snaps are the snaps with a protruding center. SOCKET snaps are the snaps that have an inverted center. The snap back is a flat piece that resembles a tack. When attaching snaps, press very firmly or the snap will not connect together properly.

JUST SO YOU KNOW....

Unless otherwise stated, all stitches are straight stitches. Yay! No crazy sewing going on here!

This page is intentionally blank

Visit www.mammacandoit.com for downloadable PDF patterns

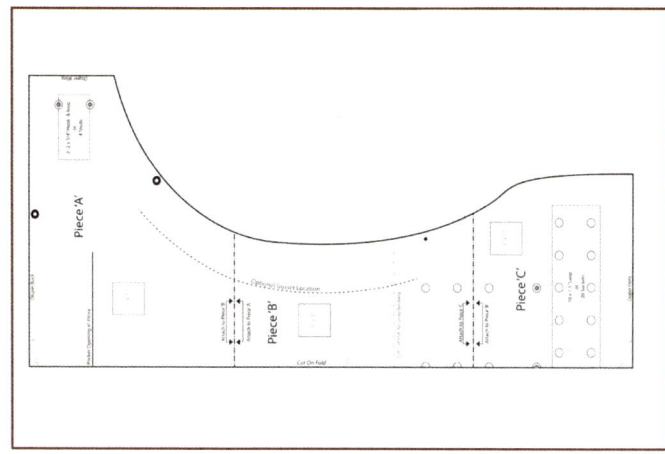

Step 1.
Print and attach pattern pieces together.

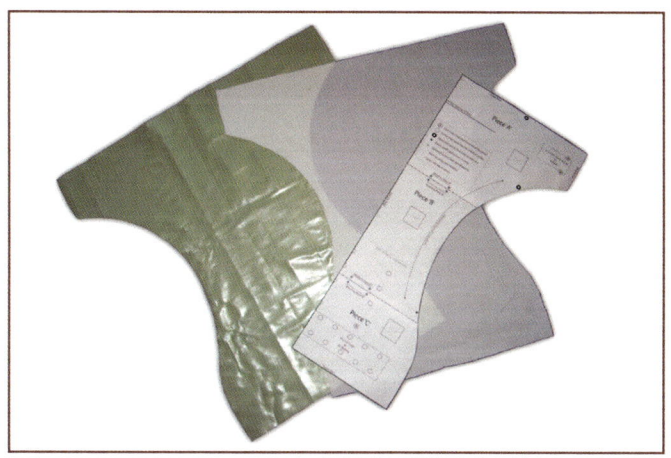

Step 2.
Cut one of PUL & alova.
These are referred to as diaper cuts throughout this tutorial.

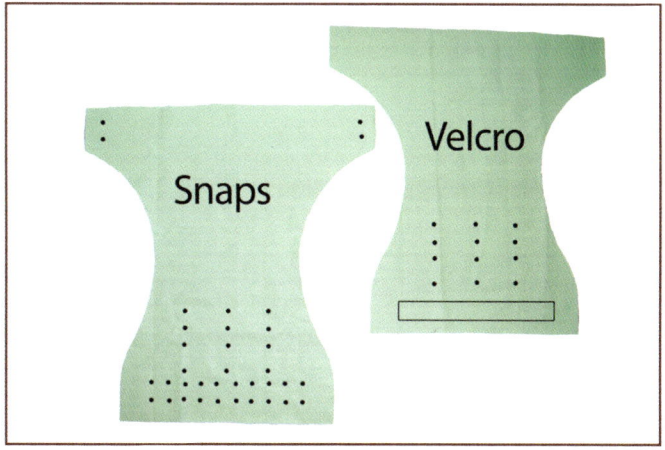

Step 3.
On the 'dull' side of the PUL diaper cut, mark all of the snap locations that you will be using.
Do this by poking a hole in the paper pattern and then marking through each hole onto the PUL.
Also mark where loop (velcro) will be if using.

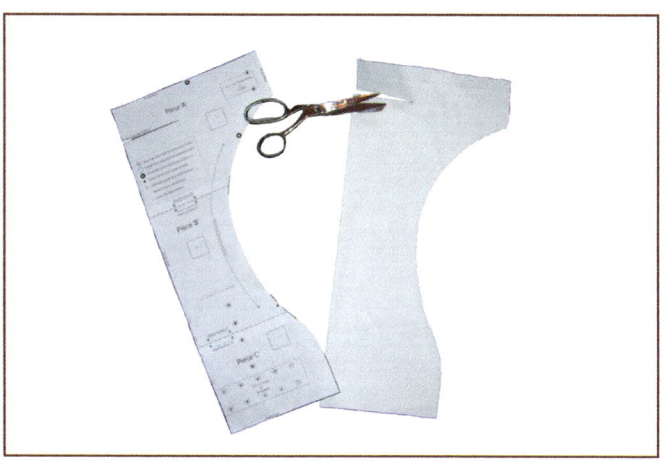

Step 4.
Fold the alova diaper cut in half and use the pattern piece to cut a slit in the top. This is for the soaker opening.
Note: Alova will not fray, so no other finishing is necessary.

This page is intentionally blank

Visit www.mammacandoit.com for downloadable PDF patterns

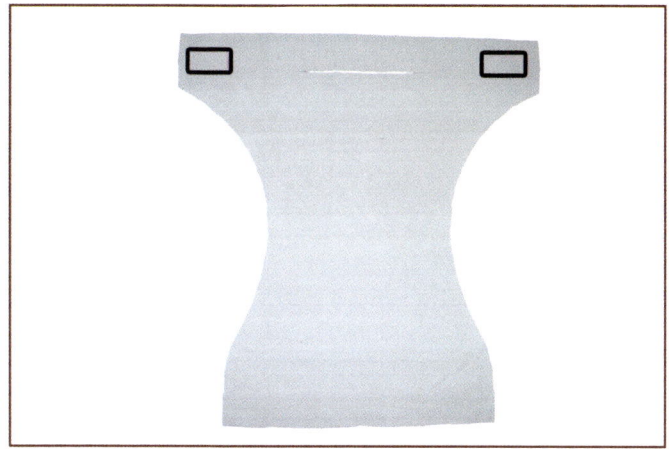

Step 5.
On the 'soft side' of the alova diaper cut, mark on the wings where the hook (velcro) will be if using velcro.

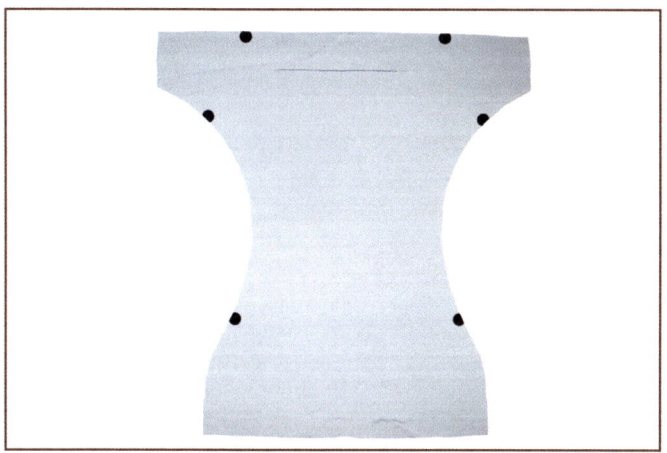

Step 6.
On the 'wrong' side of alova, mark all of the start and end locations of elastic.
See page 9 for a peak at the adjustable elastic option.

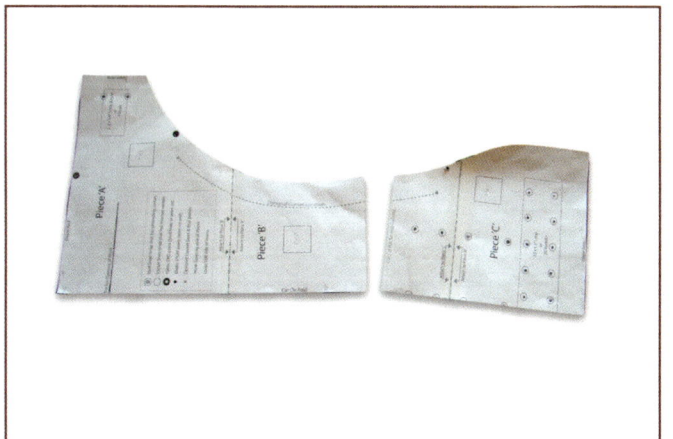

Step 7.
Cut dotted line of pattern as shown for the snap backing piece.

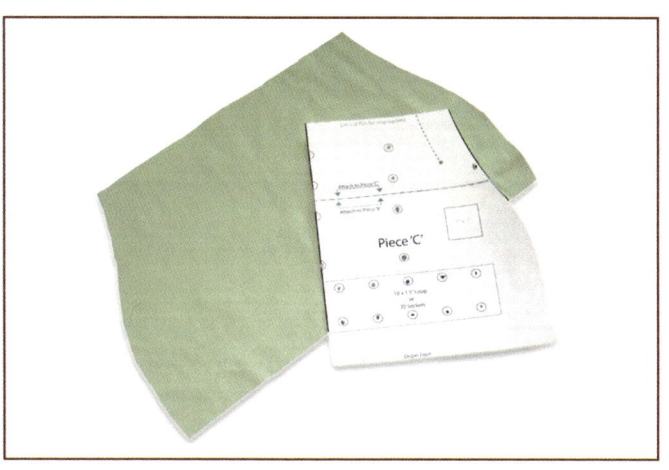

Step 8.
Cut one of PUL on the fold for snap backing.

This page is intentionally blank

Visit www.mammacandoit.com for downloadable PDF patterns

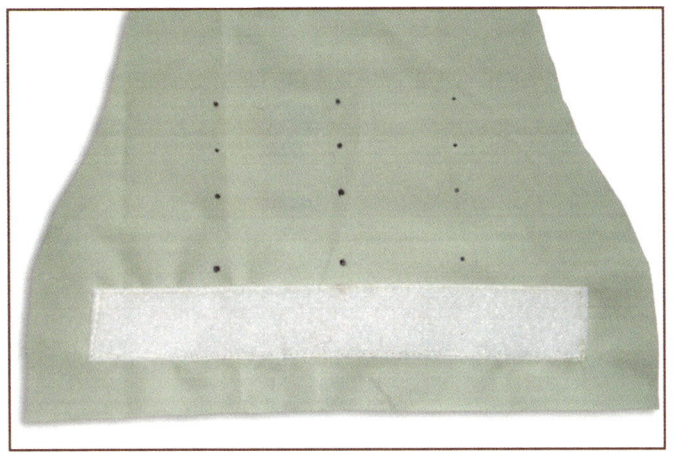

Step 9.
Sew loop (velcro) to the dull side of the PUL diaper cut using a straight stitch around entire perimeter of the loop. Do this ONLY if using velcro closure. If using snaps for closure, skip this step.

Step 10.
Attach PUL for 'snap backing' onto the "shiny" side of the PUL diaper cut. Do this by pinning, then sewing the outer edges 1/4" from the edge.
Hint: The shiny sides of PUL need to face the same direction.

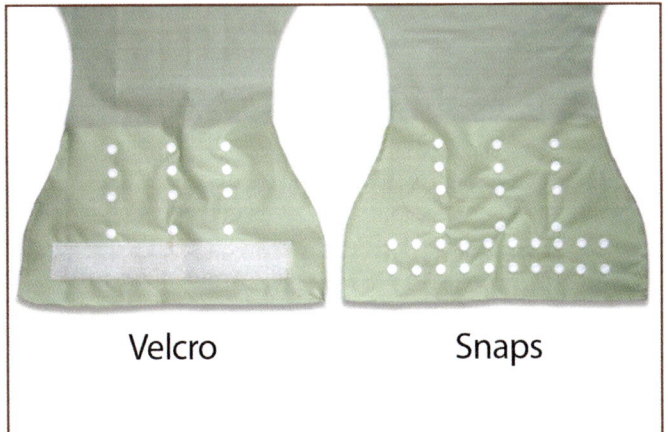

Step 11.
Attach snaps onto the front of PUL diaper cut. Do this by having the 'snapping part' of the snap on the 'dull' side of PUL. If using snaps as a closure, this would be the appropriate time to add them to the front. Do not attach snaps to wings yet.
Hint 1: Use the pattern piece to see location of studs and sockets
Hint 2: The snaps must push through BOTH layers of PUL.

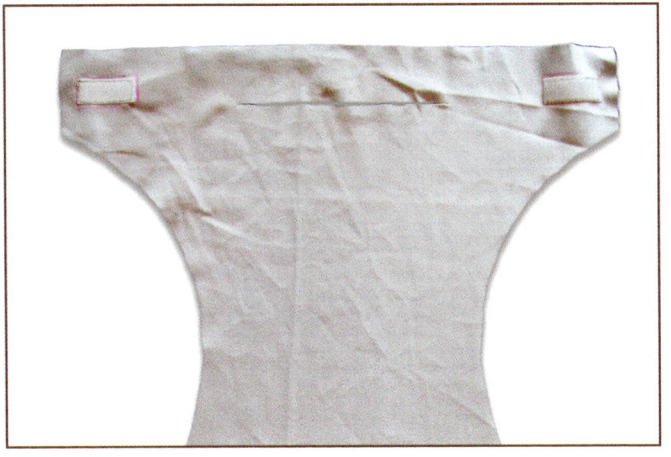

Step 12.
Attach the hook (velcro) tabs to the wings on the 'soft side' of the alova diaper cut.

6.

This page is intentionally blank

Visit www.mammacandoit.com for downloadable PDF patterns

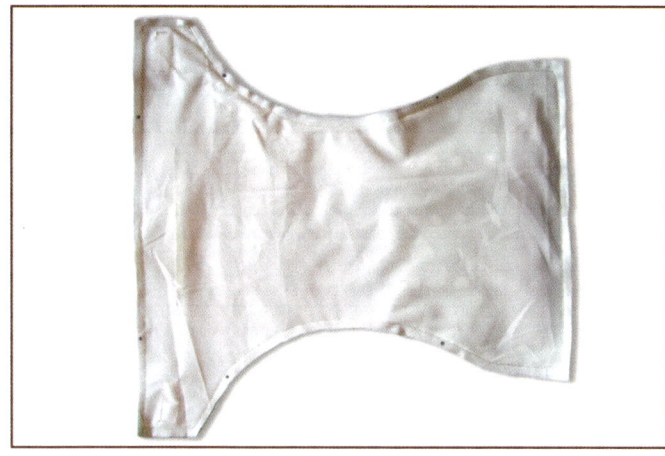

See page 9 for optional gussets tutorial.

Step 13.
Attach the alova and PUL diaper cuts together. Do this by putting the 'dull' side of PUL and the 'soft' side of alova facing together. Sew 1/2" from the edge on all edges.

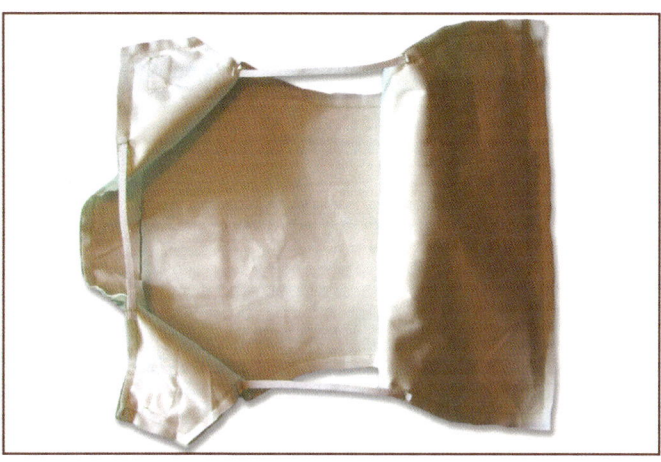

See page 11 For optional adjustable elastic tutorial.

Step 14.
Attach elastic to the alova diaper cut. On each elastic point sew the elastic onto the alova diaper cut.
Hint: Allow 1/4" of elastic to 'overhang' past the attachment seam.
Skip this step if using adjustable elastic.

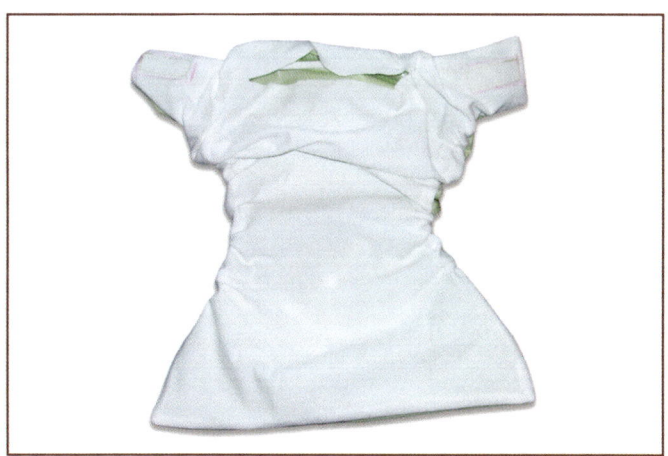

Step 15.
Turn the diaper right side out through the soaker pocket opening.

Step 16.
Create a casing for elastic in the back and legs of diaper. Pull the elastic taught while sewing slowly 1/2" from the edge of the diaper. Do NOT sew over the elastic.

Hint if using optional adjustable elastic: When sewing the casing, be sure to stop 1/2" from the 'elastic end point stud snap'.

This page is intentionally blank

Visit www.mammacandoit.com for downloadable PDF patterns

Step 17.
Sew 1/8" from the edge on all edges that do not have elastic to finish the diaper.

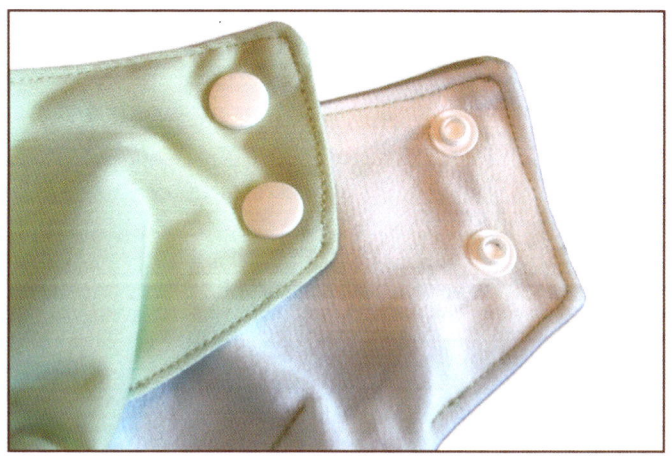

Step 18.
Attach snaps to wings if using. The 'snapping' part of the snap goes on the alova fabric.

This page is intentionally blank

Visit www.mammacandoit.com for downloadable PDF patterns

Optional Gussets
Tutorial page 1

If adding gussets to diaper, follow these steps before step 13 on page 7.

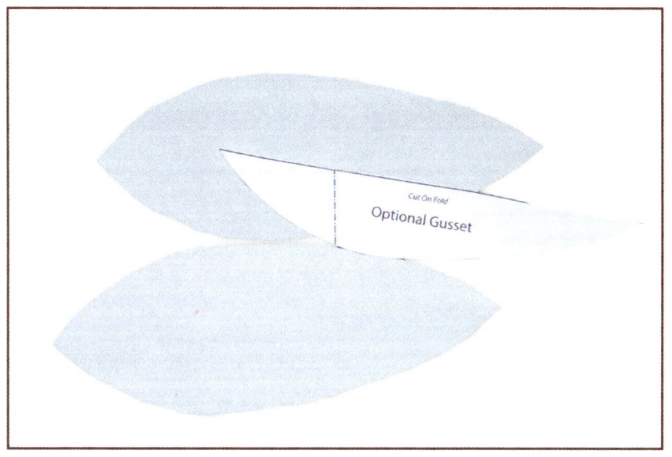

Step 1.
Cut the 'Optional Gusset' piece off of the paper pattern. Cut 2 of alova on the fold.

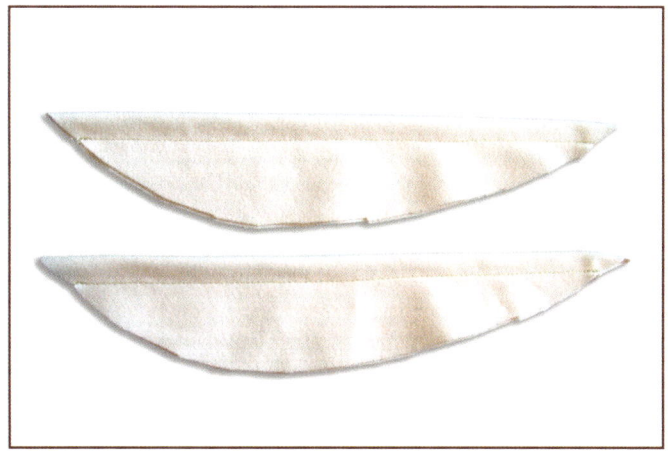

Step 2.
Keeping each gusset folded with the 'soft side' on the outside, sew 1/2" from the straight edge to create an elastic casing.

Step 3.
Cut 2 pieces of 1/4" braided elastic into 5" long pieces. Use a safety pin to 'fish them through' the elastic casings from step 2.

This page is intentionally blank

Visit www.mammacandoit.com for downloadable PDF patterns

Optional Gussets
Tutorial page 2

Step 4.
Pin and sew the elastic on each end to hold it into place.

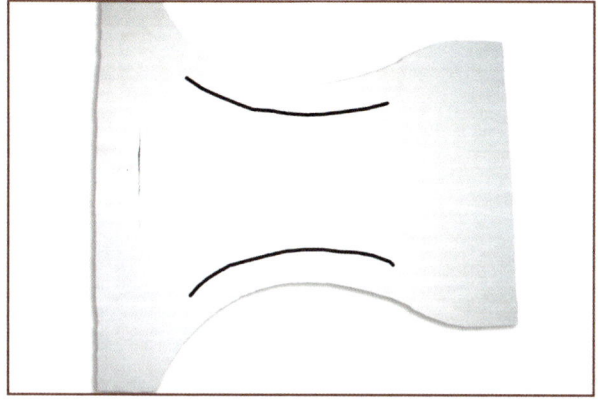

Step 5.
Use the paper diaper pattern to mark the location of gussets on the 'soft' side of alova.

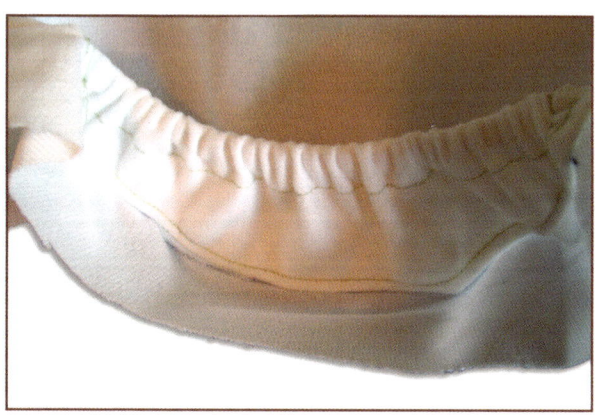

Step 6.
Lay the elastic edge of gusset toward the center of the alova. Sew the curved edge onto the mark from step 5 slowly. Sew 1/8" from the edge of the gusset. Make sure to re-enforce seam on each end.
Repeat with opposite leg.

This page is intentionally blank

Visit www.mammacandoit.com for downloadable PDF patterns

Optional Adjustable Elastic
Tutorial page 1

If adding adjustable elastic to diaper, follow these steps before step 14 on page 7.

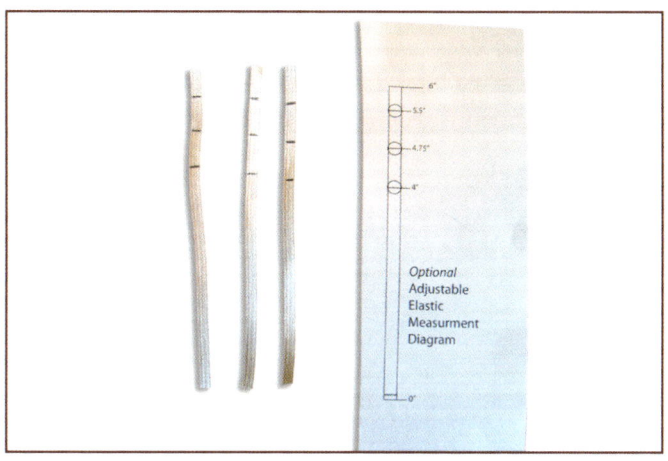

Step 1.
Cut 3 pieces of 1/4" braided elastic. Cut each piece 6" long. Use the measurement chart on page 12 to mark each piece of elastic at 4", 4.75" and 5.5".

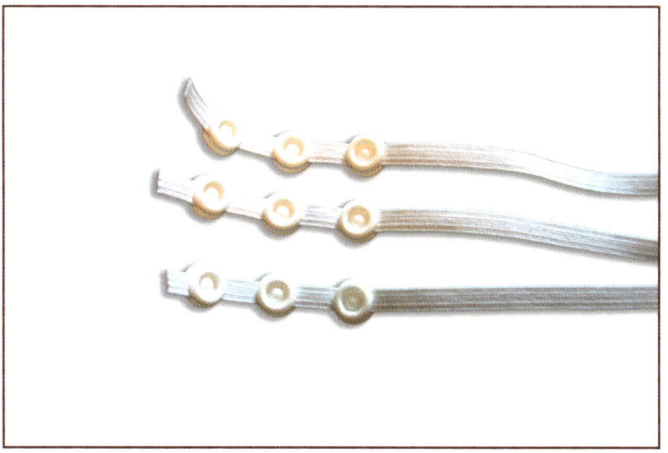

Step 2.
Attach socket snaps on each marking from previous step.

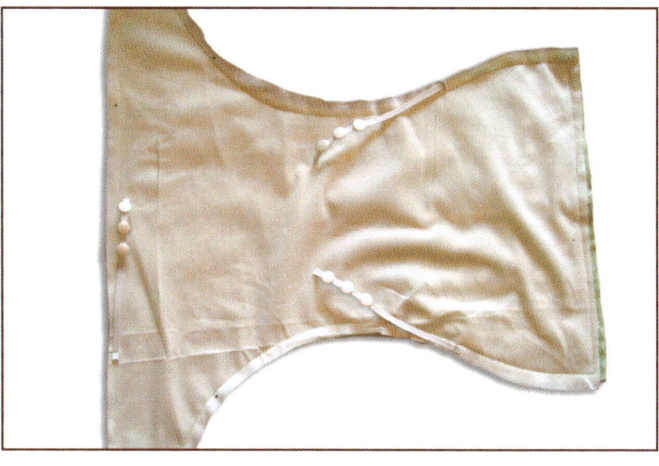

Step 3.
Attach the ends of elastic to the alova diaper cut. Make sure that the 'snapping' part of the snap is facing the diaper.

This page is intentionally blank

Visit www.mammacandoit.com for downloadable PDF patterns

Optional Adjustable Elastic
Tutorial page 2

Step 4.
Attach the stud snaps onto alova in marked location.

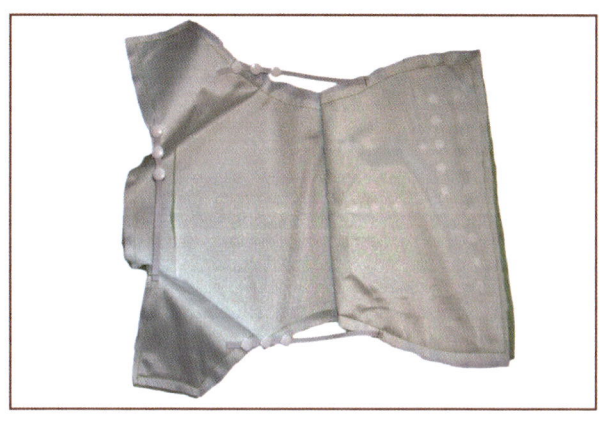

Step 5.
Attach the socket snaps onto the stud snap from previous step.

Resume page 7 on Step 15.

This page is intentionally blank

Visit www.mammacandoit.com for downloadable PDF patterns

Unlocking Creativity | You can do it.

Tips and Tricks
Useful information you just might want to know

Sewing PUL:
There is a super long list of things you can do to help sew PUL...but here is the most simple method:
The shiny side tends to stick to your presser foot...so when you are sewing PUL, sew it with the shiny side face DOWN. The feed dogs on your machine won't mind.

Attaching Snaps:
When you start attaching snaps, you'll notice that the PUL starts getting 'bunched up' a bit. The easiest remedy for this is to poke a hole through the PUL first. Use an awl or a nail to punch a hole through the PUL before setting the snap. The result: a smooth finish.

Messed up snap remedy:
The worst thing is making a 'snap' mistake. Whether putting on the wrong snap, or even placing it backwards, sometimes you need to fix it. The easiest thing to do is place the snap SIDEWAYS in the snap press and squeeze. It will break the snap. It might take a squeeze or two to come off, but it will! :) Careful planning is a must when attaching snaps.

Adjustable Elastic Casing:
When sewing the adjustable elastic casing, You'll want to stop sewing about 1/2" before the stud snap. This way you can easily adjust the diaper without the casing being in the way.

Pattern Printing:
When you print the pattern pieces, try printing on card stock! This will make a VERY durable pattern. You'll be using it over and over, so why print again and again? Try it...you'll be doing it with all of your downloaded patterns.

Snap Backing:
Yes, you need it. You're going to be snapping and unsnapping these babies quite a few times before you are through using the diapers. It not only make them more durable using a backing, but it also helps them stay LEAKPROOF!

Polyester Thread:
Don't use cotton thread when making diapers. Ever. All it will do is cause "wicking". Wicking is the term that cloth diaper users call 'leaking'. Yes....cotton thread will make your diapers leak.

Velcro tabs in the wash:
You might wonder why we didn't include velcro wash tabs in the pattern. Truthfully, it's because they never do any good. The best trick you can do is simply cut a 2x2" piece of loop velcro and attach to the soiled diaper before putting in the diaper pail. They'll stay on through the whole wash and you will always have flat tabs.

How to cut PUL: 1yd, 58-60" wide

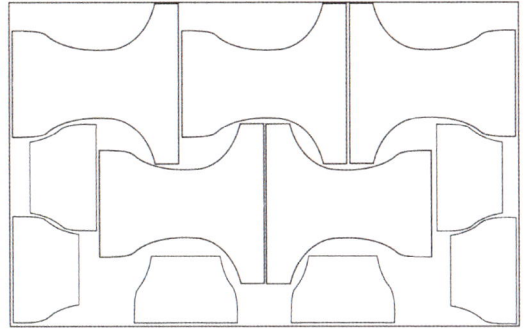

Where to buy the fabrics and supplies:
http://mammacandoit.com/articles/Sewing-Supplies-Our-favorite-places.cfm

What about a soaker:
There are two patterns available to download for free
http://mammacandoit.com/Free-Patterns/

Caring for cloth diapers:
http://mammacandoit.com/articles/Caring-for-Cloth-Diapers.cfm

13.

This page is intentionally blank

Visit www.mammacandoit.com for downloadable PDF patterns

One Size Diaper Insert
Tutorial

Copyright 2012 Mammacandoit.com

This page is intentionally blank

Visit www.mammacandoit.com for downloadable PDF patterns

Copyright 2012 Mammacandoit.com

One Size Diaper Insert
Tutorial

What you need for 8 inserts:
Microterry – 1 yd. (58-60" wide)
Bamboo Fleece- 1 yd. (40-45" wide)
Zorb - (smallest amount you can get is 1 yd)
Thread

Budget Friendly
This is our favorite fabric combination for the best absorbency for the size. You can subsitute almost anything. Try using old towels, microfiber cloths, or even flannel for some cheaper options.

Size Hint
This is our favorite size (13x13"). It absorbs about 14 oz per insert. However, if you prefer to change the size by adding length and width, you can count on about 1 oz per inch added. Example: 15x15" will get about 16 oz.

Step 1.
Cut 1 piece of microterry 14x14".
Cut one piece of bamboo fleece 14x14".
Cut 1 piece of zorb 4x13".

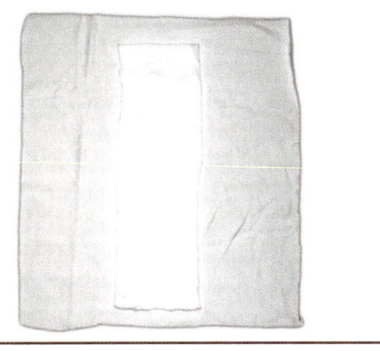

Step 2.
Layer the zorb on the center of the bamboo fleece. Make sure that the zorb is on the "NOT SOFT" side of the bamboo.

18.

This page is intentionally blank

Visit www.mammacandoit.com for downloadable PDF patterns

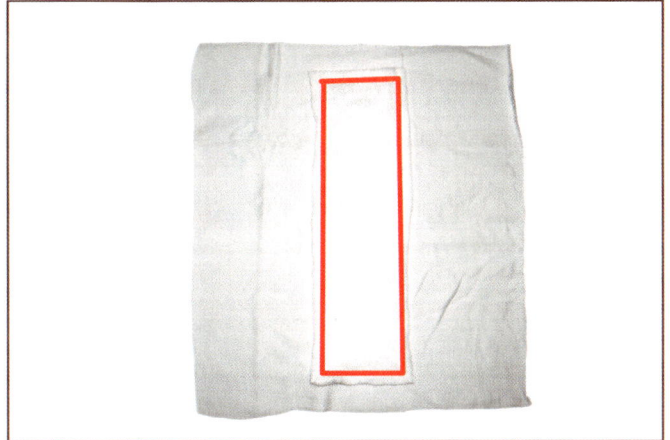

Step 3.
Sew the zorb into place 1/2" from the edge of the zorb as shown.

Step 4.
Layer the bamboo & microfiber squares together. Make sure that you layer the "soft side" of the bamboo against the microfiber.

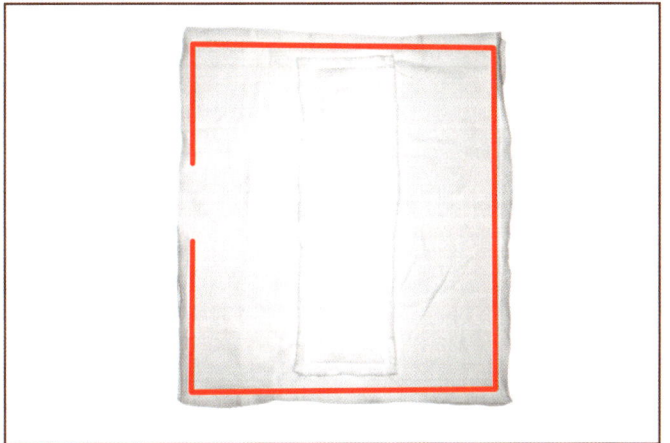

Step 5.
Sew around entire bamboo & microfiber square 1/2" from the edge. Leave a 2" opening for turning right side out.

Step 6.
Turn right side out

Step 7.
Sew the 2" opening closed about 1/8" from the edge. Then sew 1/2" from the entire perimeter to give stability to the insert.

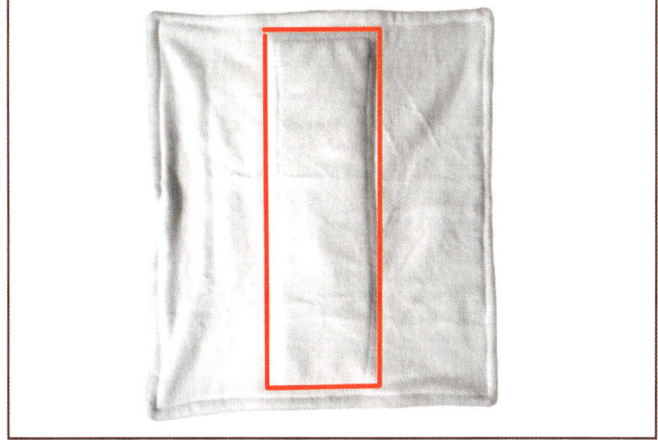

Step 8.
Use your fingers to feel where the zorb insert is. Sew around entire zorb piece to sandwich it in. This will keep the insert in place during the wash.

19.

This page is intentionally blank

Visit www.mammacandoit.com for downloadable PDF patterns